The Long Way Home

Also by John Egan and published by Ginninderra Press
Lines Continue Forever
Reworkings (Pocket Poets)
Reworkings 2 (Pocket Poets)

John Egan

The Long Way Home

Acknowledgements

Some of these poems have appeared in
The Mozzie, Ripples, Staples, Sunshine Coast Writers' Group Anthology 2007, Poetry Matters, The Write Angle, Offset, Page Seventeen, Writer's Voice, Polestar, Newswrite, Notata, Beyond the Rainbow, Five Bells, Verbatim, Signatures, Pressed, Verandah, Rust and Moth, Snorkel, The Henry Lawson Festival of Arts Anthology 2009 and *2010, Cursive Scripts Anthology 2010, Ken Again, Prospect Two, Land Lines, 21D, Kurungabaa, Velour, Valley Micropress* and *Free Expression.*

The following poems have won awards:
'On Berry Station' – 1st, 2014 Yarram Short Story & Poetry Competition
'Joe Lynch 1927' – 1st, 2013 Corinella Waterline Writing Competition
'Pluto' 1st, 2009 Siriol Kate Giffrey Literary Awards
'Gin and Tonic' – 1st, 2007 FAW North Shore Poetry Competition
'Tightrope Walking' – 1st, 2006 Circus Risky Poetry Competition, South Coast Writers Centre
'The City and the Stars – 1st, 2010 Adelaide Plains Poetry Competition
'An Idiot's Guide to…' – 1st, 2009 Yarram Community Centre Poetry Competition

For my wife Marilyn, as always.

The Long Way Home
ISBN 978 1 76041 059 9
Copyright © text John Egan 2015
Author photo: Peter Egan
Cover photo © magann

First published 2015 by
GINNINDERRA PRESS
PO Box 3461 Port Adelaide 5015 Australia
www.ginninderrapress.com.au

Contents

Walking to Newtown	9
Walking to the Writers' Festival	11
Strange Meeting	12
Leaving the Cinema	16
Then and Since and Now	17
The Mariner	18
On the Discovery of the Wreck of HMAS *Sydney*	19
The Full Moon	21
Winter Morning	23
Like a Glove	24
Water Lilies	26
The Velvet Zero	27
Terrace Houses	29
Palace Street	31
Never This Friday	32
Over the Shoalhaven	33
The Demolition of Kensington Street	34
Bricks	35
Sydney, Summer	36
Circular Quay	38
Early Autumn, Victoria Street	40
Manly	42
Facade	43
Petersham Park	44
From Wollongong to Waterfall	45
Boat Harbour – Gerringong	46
The Long Way Home	47
Reading Room	48
Rouen Cathedral	50
Autumn Leaves	51

An Idiot's Guide to…	52
My Father's Ties	53
My Father's Ties 2	54
Collected Poems	55
Hear and Do Not Hear	57
Trenchworks	59
Tightrope Walking	60
Eden Yet	62
At Berry Station	63
The Moss Vale Train	65
The City and the Stars	66
Disappointment	67
The Winds of August	68
Morning's Symphony	69
Headlines	71
Pluto	72
Angels Embracing	74
This Church	76
The *Californian*	**77**
Downstream	84
Water	85
The Noise the Silence Makes	87
Old Ships	89
Journey to the Renal Ward	93
Respiratory Ward	95
Blood Test	97
Kidney Stone	98
A. Cooke	100
Autumn and Darkness	101
The Tango Dancers	102
Two Young Soldiers	104
Snake Lady	105

For Panadda	106
Gin and Tonic	107
Who Did You Say?	108
Floating	110
Time	111
The Song	112
Joe Lynch 1927	113
Walking to Redfern	116

Walking to Newtown

The long lonely down Wilson Street,
mellow brick and walls
that shoulder the shambles away
and carriage sheds, artefacts
of steam and manufacture,
industrial construction that rides
like a cathedral in the Romanesque
above the piles of rubble,
among a wasteland of tin.
Rows of terrace houses
like reconfigured molars
in the gentle jaws
of Eveleigh and Darlington.

The brilliant green of plane trees
that billow in the wind
to second floors of wrought-iron
and a colour-chart of cars
that nose each other
like piglets in the street
or buzz like children's toys
a glide and whirr
along the tree-lined afternoon –
a larger quality of gone
and fast dimensions
beyond the sound of breath –
my footfall repetition
of asphalt under shoes.

The direct route
to Newtown's shops and noise.
A coffee there and raisin toast,
though really there's no reason
for me to go –
I walk because I can,
because I like to walk
and keep on walking
now I'm here –
while here is comfortable and nice,
I'm travelling on to there,
that enigmatic somewhere else, the prize
that dances teasingly ahead,
that once was here
but never is here now.

This warm and solitude,
this afternoon that slides itself to evening,
I walk the kilometres
in the minutes and the hours,
although occasionally the sense
that all those years could be,
silent, mellow, enormous,
slowly walking me.

Walking to the Writers' Festival

I amble across a neat, hardwood bridge,
a tourist walkway to rows of finger wharves.
An archway through massive, Edwardian
brick and dock, industrial form
and function – apartments, restaurants, shops,
gentrified, rebuilt, the former Walsh Bay piers.

Forty years ago it wasn't here. A boy,
I watched the swing of cranes and derricks, heard
the whine of winches and the clang of steel
as holds of ships were emptied, freight on pallets,
a myriad of nets and ropes. Here,
the high, sharp bows of cargo ships
reared themselves, their anchors clenched like knots
on the muscles of their hulls.

They'd cut the waves from Hamburg and Rotterdam
to unload here, where I quietly stroll.
Forty years ago – freighters and their cargoes.
Here, exactly here.

Strange Meeting

A vast new sea, empty and dangerous as the moon.
An unknown coast, southern Terra Australis,
either New Holland or New South Wales.
Were they the same? No gulf, no waters
to separate the two. The only ship, her provisions
low, fresh water always the scourge,
perennial as death on this alien coast,
the only settlement a lifetime to the east,
through Bass Strait and somewhere to the north.
Like a speck on the edge of nowhere
and winter approaching.

Lieutenant Matthew Flinders, commander,
HMS *Investigator*, a season east
of King George Sound, New Holland, a month
out of Spencer Gulf, and there was no inland sea,
a few day's sail from Kangaroo Island,
made the only decision he could: interrupt
his great voyage, sail direct to Sydney,
re-provision and repair his ship, refresh his crew,
his own health and spirits, then sail again
to explore this new land he'd personally called Australia.

A shout from the lookout, a white rock in the sea?
A pyramid? An obelisk? Then 'Ship ahoy –
a sail!' A ship coming west towards them,
a ghost direct from the planet Mars. No
top-gallants raised, but heavy, three hundred tons,
a frigate like themselves, but who? And are we still
at war with France? Raise a white flag – truce.
Most of her cannons gone, removed for space and science,
Investigator was still a British man-o'-war.
No response. What reply to a white flag? Surrender?
So raise the British flag, the pennant,
the Union Jack, and then the end of mystery.
La Geographe responded, her colours French,
but were they still at war? April 1802,
neither knew of the peace Treaty of Amiens,
ten months since leaving Portsmouth, so
'Clear for action – action stations.' Prepare
for battle at the end of the world.

Captain Nicholas Baudin, six months out of the east coast
of Van Diemen's Land, nineteen months from France,
his mission identical, to explore and chart
the coastline of New Holland, to solve the mystery:
one continent or two? Already Flinders knew
there was no strait, just Terra Australis,
but Baudin had yet to see the Great Australian Bight,
its cliffs hundreds of feet and on the whole arc
and track no mouth of any river.
His ship swung slowly at the frigate,
his approach slow and sinister as the age of the earth.

In his great cabin, Baudin criticised
his maps of Van Dieman's Land, had
no idea the man who drew them was his guest.
Flinders knew of Baudin's voyage
but the Frenchman knew nothing of him.
Younger, ill at ease, Baudin easily outranked him.
Baudin spoke no English, Flinders no French, so a stilted,
translator-driven dialogue, an awkward meeting,
and then a sharing of information, of maps,
narratives of ordeals, of accidents,
good men drowned, boats lost, scurvy, hunger, thirst.

The next day, he knew who Flinders was,
acknowledged his pleasure in meeting him,
the gallantry of gentlemen.
The ships departed, west and east, lonely seabirds
on a lonely quest. Eighteen months later
Baudin was dead of stress and disease,
the strain of leadership, of years at sea.
He was barely fifty. Never returned to France.
Flinders was away over nine years, six
restrained by the French, a prisoner of war
and never put to sea again,
died at home, old at forty.

The place of their meeting is Encounter Bay.
They both failed to see, hidden by miles of sand dunes
the mouth of Australia's largest river,
not five miles from where they spoke. They drew
new maps of the continent and moulded
the shape we know, rivals who briefly met
and sailed on, flawed heroes of the sea
and the builders of coastlines.

Leaving the Cinema

It's no-man's-land, shell-cratered with the shock
of having left but not arrived, borders
unclaimed like the wounded and the dead
who can't be heard and can't be found.
There's disbelief before you own the light,
adjust from two dimensions into flesh,
poor buggered reality, touch your life
again, stare and blink – leave the theatre dazed.

A film of murder, mystery and ghosts,
the foyer lights are merciless on tat,
a lonely mansion on the Spanish coast
and then Toyotas queued in Norton Street.
It's waking from a dream or out of love
that shrinks bright worlds to diagrams in black.

Then and Since and Now

Searching for the house my parents
almost bought fifty years ago,
I thought I'd recognise the street
it should've been, almost the spot
it could've stood but wrong and wrong –
nought remains of what I thought
was there, but isn't now, my memory twisted
by the Once, overlain with Since.

Facts corrode forgotten seasons,
a million heartbeats, decades after Then.
Years cascade into cycles of rain and sleep.
The warp of timbers and the rust
of precision melt your sharpness
into platitude and fuzz,
disconnect the exact
from what is Here and Now.

Memoirs give way to narratives
and myth, history reconfigures
to a legend in the mind, phantoms
and foundations synapsed so tightly
into fact that Then receded
gently into Wrong.

The Mariner

Navigate your frail Whitby barque
in the trade winds of the day
and the soft horizons of tomorrow,
across the meridians of months
and the parallels of years.
A cartographer of decades
the ship's log your life's diary, your charts
the scars notched in mind and muscle.
Your bruises sprawl in verse and rhyme
and the white page is stressed with waves
in the wake of your voyages. Wind blown
to the high latitudes of time
where the ice ticks loudly like a clock,
the polestar beckons north
and all directions merge to here.
There is no compass
and then there is no light.

On the Discovery of the Wreck of HMAS *Sydney*

Grey gladiator,
chopped to death
in the silent stadium
of the bloody sea.

Broken warrior,
bleeding the mystery
of waves and years.

A thin ghost
smashed to smoke,
the memories
of wives and daughters

who waved goodbye
as you steamed away
over horizons
of endless waiting,

commands given
in battles
no one saw
and lived.

And now
radar pinpoints
the privacy
of steel and bone.

What wreckage
and the answers
to what questions?
To what ends?

The Full Moon

The trees are naked to the wind,
the road's a woven scarf
flung between the garden and the hills.

The moon's hollow eye,
ivory in the night, against the stars
like a perfect crystal – craters, valleys,
and her desiccated seas of dust.

A face in a glassless window,
a mansion, stately once,
derelict and abandoned but for ghosts
in empty rooms and long corridors
of lonely, rotting stars.

The moon's a haunted woman,
mesmerised in her garden,
thick with weeds and fallen tree limbs,
the ruins of a staircase, cracks
in crumbling masonry and broken urns.

On naked shoulders, around her white neck,
a scarf of ebony, knotted
like a shackle, soft as satin,
hard as bitumen and her eyes staring,
silver, deep, unearthly
as her old enemy the midday sun.

The road reflects the embers
in her eyes and weaves like a monody
from the cities of the past,
the cycles of tides and the birth of days,
evenings by the fire, the heat-death of stars.

It curves towards the future,
rises from the moon's memory,
above the sullen trees to the black,
unknown hills, fathomless as the sea.

Winter Morning

The morning's edge of here.
Great glacial ships of ice
and gravestorms in ice-veins, icicle spars
like mirrors on a lake.
Ice-dragons blur in slurries of snowskin,
blue caves and filaments of light.

Skybodies drift like handfuls of the sea
and skeletons in fingerfuls of wind.
Morning sprawls in the tidal air,
the spindled trees, fear-edged the sinister,
the bare-boned willows, the barebacked river
drags a cloak of memory and mist.

A listless procession, the pleated creek
drives the morning and the ice
like the black spider's blackened web.
Morning crawls from sleep to wake
among the relics of the sea and the sun's
black petticoats of ash.

Like a Glove

It's midnight and the stench of dark.
Rain sizzles from the humid street,
sobs in the gutter and clips the leaves,
a cyclic, heartbeat drip at night
and the slow ebb of youth to skeletons
of time in digital, in analogue, numbers
that click to small. Clocks rotate like
suns that will not burn forever.

Lucinda Williams sings elegies to loss,
pricks the skin where the dank bones knit,
her husky songs that flirt with death.
Her answer is submission to the pain,
wear your anger like a cloak,
spread your hand like a sharp-edged knife.
Some laws should be broken from the start, be
the traitor and the thief, a broken butterfly –
songs that scour the essence of regret.

The past shatters the present like a god.

A fan revolves inside its cage, a lamp
scatters colour, graffitis the swollen page
with spiderwebs of thought, emblems of speech
loop to unplanned worlds and words of songs
pass only into air, the bow-waves of liners
hissing up the scrap yard beach, blowtorch
mudflats in the south of Bangladesh.
Their lights diminish, worlds diminish, songs
reduced to slivers of plastic, CDs
spun in moody cycles, rhymes in the dark, sorrow
clicked to silence. There is no motive and no aim.
Rain spins the wake of doomed liners
that fold the horizon like a glove.

Water Lilies

Claude Monet, 1907, Museum of Fine Arts, Boston

There is no earth, there is no sky,
only the fertile water's flow.
Limitless the focus of the eye

and limitless the water's sigh.
A surface of leaves and flowers.
There is no earth, there is no sky.

A water world bedazzled by
a sun-glanced and reflected glow.
Limitless the focus of the eye.

Lilies of pink, a summer flies
and glistened leaves are clumped as though
there is no earth, there is no sky.

The leaves are pathways as they lie.
From drifting rafts the blossoms grow.
Limitless the focus of the eye.

The world's a liquid lullaby,
in patterns sunlight dances so
there is no earth, there is no sky.
Limitless the focus of the eye.

The Velvet Zero

Beyond the desk lamp,
its green shade,
the multiple slash
of sharp venetians
and the shrouded night
that covers knots of trees
and walls of rough brick
with nothing,
the void,
the velvet zero
clicking into time and space,
spinning into now.

Densities of dark matter
and the energy of stars
that drive the universe
to eternity's abyss.

Anchored to a small star,
we measure the precision of plastic
and the significance of paper
among moments that explode
into no one, nothing, nowhere.

Beyond the known filament of trees
I've touched but cannot see,
a clump of thin, white light,
the midnight doorway to the building
across the hollow, an alien sun
whose light we see rushing from the past,
a pinprick source, the period
that drives to Doppler red,
accelerates to what-might-be-there
and particles of spin,
light years from the stars
that may not
even be there now.

Terrace Houses

Behind the filigree and ironwork fences
jasmine droops and curls around
the balcony, the gateway and the dirty,
unswept tiles, a narrow porch and railing
of one door in this long, forbidding row
of nineteenth-century terrace houses.

Between the gateway and the doorway
a small and private patio,
an outdoor, halfway space to ponder,
not vestibule or waiting room
nor purgatory nor hell.

Push the gate, enter, knock
and wait there for the door to open.
Notice ugly pipes and plumbing,
the nasty criss-cross apparatus
of electrical and gas supply.
A bike or garbage tip, a ragged stack
of floor mats, neatly piled, sinister
and strange, left to rot there, just below
the graceful, late-Victorian sill.

Wait until the opened door invites you.
Enter rooms with people, laughter,
speech and choices, acts, decisions –
rooms in red with old, black curtains,
a narrow staircase to the second floor.

But should the door refuse to open,
take the footpath, take the street,
walk the desolate and lesser highways
that lead you to obscure horizons,
to dry lakes, deserts, tracks of saltbush,
unclouded suns that flatter and can kill.

Some who never brave that entrance, never
risk the chill and choices, the sweating
on the distressed, brown and gritty tiles
walk the ghost-roads and their voices
linger long and sullen faces, phantoms
on the rainswept empty street.

Every terrace house I've known
has an entry much like this one.
Some have jasmine in the doorway,
most do not.

Palace Street

Cars precisely skirt the roundabout.
Neat terrace houses jostle into rows
and coyly hide their need for paint.
Every lime-green jacaranda

now bustles to restrain itself
from bursting into flower
and like a schoolboy makes a show
to stand there, disciplined and quaint.

The street inclines exactly up the hill,
staid, brick fences and bungalows that match
and here a planned decline and bob
towards the railway and its station.

The village simmers in the afternoon.
Its small suburban hum vibrates
with energy imprisoned there.
Overhead, jets repress the strident air.

Never This Friday

Traffic swarms through the square.
Buses slow and stop.
Passengers climb or step or jump.
The old stump post office building
commands the morning
and its place.

The railway clock tower
spins the hours
in stone and brick.

Another Friday
cool and wet,
like any Friday yes,
but never this Friday,
not this one
ever again.

Over the Shoalhaven

A mosquito-buzzing drone
brooding eastwards into night.
Cramped steerage in the belly of a Boeing,
waiting as the air miles wind themselves
tediously back to home and morning.
Two a.m. in transit at K.L.
then lightning scours the Timor Sea.

Vectored south of Sydney,
a wide sweep to the morning's ocean flight path,
dipping westward into Kingsford Smith.
A hollow hemisphere of land and space
floating here among the sunburst blue,
a wild clarity of light
crashing into kilometres
of air and height
the sprawl of endless greeneries,
archaic bush and rock.

A wilderness,
ancient, mysterious and home.
The ribs and shoulders
of turtle mountain Coolangatta.
The blue serpent, thin Shoalhaven
also winds homeward to the sea –
the lifeblood, body and the face
of what and who I am
and where I'm meant to be.

The Demolition of Kensington Street

Where the walls once stood, now there's only sky.
The warehouse that defined this street has gone.
The past is rubble and is left to lie,

the quiet and tranquil time gone by
collapsed to space and vacancy and sun.
Where the walls once stood, now there's only sky.

Mouldering and timeless, the brickwork dried
with age and shadows to a mellow tongue.
The past is rubble and is left to lie,

the present roars and rattles with the cry
of drills and cranes, the hard hats, hammers swung.
Where the walls once stood, now there's only sky

and panes of windows, splintered, dangling eyes,
beams and scaffolds, archways, steel-coils flung.
The past is rubble and is left to lie.

The street is naked to the wind, the sigh
of crowds who do not know or care it's gone.
Where the walls once stood, now there's only sky.
The past is rubble and is left to lie.

Bricks

A work of art in common clay,
shades of the real earth's subtle colours.
Textures compressed in seams of rock,
ancient bone of sand and forest.

Every brick is slightly different,
walls of touch and layers scraped,
variety and scope within the same
restrictions on their size and shape.

Portraits of every age and epoch
born in fire and cool-string matched, rows
of permanence and style. Sydney's
soul is laid with brick, not made of stone.

Sydney, Summer

Walls and fences of the darkest brick
draw the heat, sunlight smeared like blood
on footpaths, asphalt, streets. The thin houses
hide their cunning, hoard their stash
behind verandas and doors that smile.
The false modesty of curtains.
Chain-gang origins and their later lies,
facades of the respectable and good.

The light boils sandstorms on the road.
The heat's a club rips your eyes, the brain
split like robbery. Shade and shadows
guard the sun, tall assassins,
hooded, vigilant, impenetrable
and never wholly seen or fully there
but hard as henchmen in the afternoon,
enforce some contract, rule or whim.

The sun beats an ancient corroboree
along the circle of its day.
The stomp and gnarl of heat, crescendos
in its blind and burn, dust in tread and drum.
The light collapses into shrill.
Walk with eyes half shut. Yellow merges into black
behind your lids, the ache of midday burned
to dark, pulses into flecks and vertigo.

The butcher boys of heat, the thugs of summer
have broad arrows on their suits, their backs
and knuckles white with scars, the bruises
marked in centigrade and sweat. Pale felons
sentenced to February or for life,
this colony of punishment and fire.
They pine for autumn and relief.
The sun keeps spitting like a wrecking ball.

Circular Quay

A rain-lashed Quay
and white-wine footsteps splashed to spray.

Commuters crabwalk and the wind
defeats their umbrellas.
Sullen ferries, tightly moored,
huddled to the wharf,
dishwater-flat the harbour
and Utzon's sails, humpbacked,
scraped with grey,
surrender into mist.

The bridge dissolves a latticework
of arches, mellow laces
melting into cloud. The city softened
bends to grey.

Small, impulsive as a yacht,
the *Narrabeen* steams ferociously
past the mass of Bennelong
and dropping down from fourteen knots,
slows to green-hulled
yellow upperworks and home
from Manly, the far exotic sea,
glides to berth at Jetty Two
with all the grace and wide aplomb
of Cunard's *Berengaria*
or White Star Line's *Olympic*
at Manhattan's Lower West side piers.

Old photos
shot in black and white –
the elevated roadway
and the Hudson River docks,
the 1920s North Atlantic Ferry,
for a moment bring
Jazz-Age glamour, Old World style
even here,
a continent and whole Pacific,
eighty years away –
the rain-soaked
grey and windy Quay.

Early Autumn, Victoria Street

Autumn touches the plane trees
with a gentle reminder.
Their leaves are turning brown.
They're again starting to fall.

Twice I've walked this tree-lined street
looking for the house I first
came to thirty years ago.
I can't be sure I've found it.

Every second building's now
a hostel for backpackers.
The mysterious staircase
I remember twisting down

from the elegant front room
is now the corner of a small office.
The house seemed so much larger then
both inside and out.

It's thirty years – buildings change
and memory changes buildings.
They're not the same building
in reality or time and even now

it's hard to know what's changed the most,
the world or me. It was
usually evening when I came here
but now it's early afternoon.

I remember my thirty-year-old self,
a different person in values,
experience, ideals – naive then, more
optimistic, a vast future stretching

into a clear, blue sky forever.
The gentle breeze and autumn again
threaten to change everything I know.
I've finished my coffee. It's time to go.

Manly

South Steyne, 7 a.m.

Pine trees
line the esplanade,
tall as hotels.
Green verticals
scratch the clouds,
scrape across dull horizons.
Colours melt,
the morning's hollow hues
wash to iron.
Creases of waves
beaten flat
by grey whips of rain.

Joggers run with dogs,
juggling domes.
Umbrellas spill stripes and colours
like buttons onto a grey vest.
Brown-washed trunks
bend to ranks and columns.
Curves of verticals
shelter under torrents,
canopies and cones
kissed by the rain.
Files of foliage, whole promenades
of horizontals –
the great, glistening, green rollers
of trees.

Facade

The building's empty facade,
behind is nothing
but rusting girders braced
against the old streetscape

and its face of bricks and paint.
At night, space supports the moon
through glassless window frames
and skeletons of faded signs.

The stars enclosed by walls,
neglected grass and weeds
once were offices and corridors
where only the cats glide now,

as if ownership has fallen
from conformity and order
to the wildness of vacancy
in a prison of bricks and bars.

Behind the facade new stars burn
and cats, ignorant
of law and civilisation
sparkle like creatures of the air.

Petersham Park

Even the wind feels different.
There's space to build momentum,
to rev the isobars and blow
like an Airbus sweeping up the sky.

The air's greener and the grass is cool
and a neat avenue of trees
stands strictly to attention, a mark
of genuine respect as you walk by.

A visitor of gravitas and style,
you snap returns to their salutes,
inspect the features of their park –
the children's playground's sharp vibration

and a corroboree of dogs,
the benches set in facing rows
and after the jumbled, toy-box houses
jostled in the street, air and space and light.

From Wollongong to Waterfall

A filament of bitumen that spears
the bush, black as paragraphs
in print. Shadow-thickened trees, the road signs
like hieroglyphs, materialise, swell
to sinister. Syllables of giant's speech,
immense the now that flicks
to nothing and the past.

A highway rolls directly into then.
Cars accelerate on headlight beams.
The diphthong lanes of roadway rhyme with light
and tenses going forward into fast.

The distant specks of twin-red traffic
fade to stanzas in a poem, spin
in kilometres, whisper into space.
The roadsong language of the car
becomes a ballad made of time and here.

Boat Harbour – Gerringong

Below the cliff the sea's moaning at your feet.
Wave crests waver into space, planet high,
slab-sided, ocean rollers batter in from the moon,
race in columns and rows, heave themselves to death,
explosions of spray, exhalations of foam-burst,
a juggernaut assault, the weight and bulk
of wet tonnage shudders onto walls of rock.

Basalt tiles, weathered by salt and tide,
crack to a neatness of squares, rank by rank
their edges curled by run-off, the sun's heat
after the freeze and scrape, the swell and ram,
unseen seepage, inundation of drops
swollen into rock, carnage caused
by trickle-down and slop.

Rock face scoured by sand and wind, sparse grasses
and the runnelled heath cling in spite of squall
and spray and the deadly kiss of salt.

Watch the death of waves, the sea's onslaught
against the world. Investigate rock-pools
in their warmth and cosiness. Jump
from platform to shell-drift. Step on
channels and cracks, alien as
canals on Mars, tiny life forms
strange as air, ferocious as the sun.
Hear the rattle of pebbles, the stealth
of the wind that urges on the waves –
a dark wind that strokes the sea, cools the humid rocks
and breaks each wave to jetsam and to tears.

The Long Way Home

for Henry Lawson

Walk the long way home, turn right
past the neo-gothic stones,
Sydney Mortuary Station,
and right at Queen or Meagher.

Wander the small streets north of Cleveland,
tree-lined and quiet, backwater
warehouses of the late nineteenth century,
apartments now or offices.

The coffee shop on Abercrombie
and The Kastle, innocuous
in a row of run-down terraces,
verandas precarious as grace.

The hill that looms up suddenly
to the vacant hump of the railway bridge –
opposite's the longer, shallow rise
to Victoria Park and City Road.

The long way home through dingy streets
and lines of door-stop houses, bumping
their shoulders, shuddering on to Redfern,
to Darlington and the west.

Walk the long way home where the city
and the nearest suburbs meet,
a history of buildings, the narrative
of lives in every face in every street.

Reading Room

After the racket of the swirling Quay,
three blasts from the harbour ferry –
'Watch out. I'm going fast astern',
it's always quiet and calm in here.

Old and sage, here's a mid-Victorian
tradition of clear respect for dignity
and learning through the written word,
the solitude of silent contemplation.

Tables of polished brownwood fill the room
and simple reading lamps of cream.
Dark-stained shelves, Reference and Fiction.
Book-spines ranked in a Dewey uniform

of neatness and precision, catalogued and classified,
their titles lucid in the formal sun,
red and black the *Cambridge Ancient History*
and the great, brooding *Oxford Dictionary of English*.

An occasional, murmured word or phrase,
the flick of turning pages, the rustle
of notes and paper imply intense
solidity and depth, a darker quality

of will, emphasised by muffled coughs
and the humiliation of a sneeze,
the rigid aura of struggle and control.
Tight in desperate confrontation,

figures still as carvings, the hours
of sheer determination, each reader,
his fierce and private wrestling with
the stubborn, thick brutality of text.

Rouen Cathedral

Morning Effect, Claude Monet, 1894

The blue bulk of facade,
the mass of the west front
shoulders out of the yellow mist
and shimmers into morning.

Monet painted the cathedral –
nuances of light and shade,
day and season –
thirty times until he dreamed

the stones collapsed around him
and buried in rubble
radiated hues
of blue and pink and yellow.

I examine my desk lamp
with its green shade and golden base,
the white fan and the open window –
lift the blue Parker once again…

Autumn Leaves

The painter Hokusai
was summoned
by the emperor
to paint at court,
a brilliant honour.

He dipped the foot of a chicken
into the blue paint
and dragged it gently
over a long scroll
of rice paper.

He took the feet
of a live bird,
placed them
into vermilion ink
and let the chicken
walk across the scroll.

After this was done
he bowed deeply
to his royal patron
and displayed the work
many regard as his
greatest achievement.
He called it
Autumn Leaves
Falling on the Yangtze

An Idiot's Guide to…

Poems are not created,
they're discovered
enveloped in darkness,
obscured in the depths
of your mind,
like diamonds
they lie there
waiting
and all your drafting,
editing, reworking
is just to coax them
into the glare
of the open page.

They squirm naked
and vulnerable
in the heat
of your concentration
until they've grown
in confidence,
demand to be noticed,
cry to be read
and learn to crave
the spotlight and the audience,
like actors who might survive,
might succeed,
like grown children
no longer yours.

My Father's Ties

My father told stories that were almost true.
His wild, wide Irish tongue shaped the world
and always found an angle, made the worst
of all defeats sound just fantastic.

I'm not like him: I find
the nastiness behind the smiling face –
the funnel-web in the old boot.
I connect the spider to the foot,
the foot to the stair and the stair
to the cellar where the old things are
I keep but do not need.

My father's ties, the ones he wore to work
and when he died I took, although
I never wear a tie.
I see them long and multicoloured
like carpets or ribbons or snakes.

I cannot give them away.
Like my father's stories they've become mine.
I've never worn one, never.
My father's stories. My father's ties.
My poems have become almost never false.

My Father's Ties 2

My father's ties in the garage
are like my poems – coloured things
dredged from the unconscious,
at first smeared and filthy, foul and dark,
but then I work on them – a little washing,
a little rubbing and a snip here,
stitching there and they might be
presentable, might be readable,
might work.

But they're never really mine.
They come from him and before him
his parents and their ancestors.
All our ancestors.

I only connect the unconnectable.

The light from a poor star
that's travelled
an infinity of years
from the edge of the galaxy
connects us all.

Collected Poems

The poet, dead now
thirty years,
looks down, confident and calm,
directly at the camera.

His face a study
of middle-age and wisdom,
strength and competence.
Behind round, black glasses,

his thoughtful gaze
(chin on hand, lips
slightly compressed
by a relaxed knuckle)

looks fixedly at us,
half a lifetime later.
The knowledge, energy and power
of twentieth-century America.

A few books lie tumbled
on the white bookcase
behind his neat,
black, receding hair,

fashionable and short.
Half his lifetime spent
crumpled in depression,
in and out of mental institutions,

despite the status
of his birth and family.
The cover of *Collected Poems*,
his portrait lifted, as it says,

from *Life* magazine.
His life is here.
His most famous poem
tells of imprisonment

Hear and Do Not Hear

It's not the striking of the bell
in the cold, silent room.
It's the echo that lingers
and the sounds you never hear.

It's not the thing that's done
but the echoes of what was done
that linger in the mind.
They hang in the silent air,
in the later lives of those
who do not listen or will not hear.

The whine of twin-jet
Pratt and Whitneys spooling up
to keep that Boeing in the air –
a final approach on water
before its landing here.

I hear the end of fourteen hours
they've spent hanging in the air,
the echoes of bells were striking
for the passengers up there
and the echoes that brought them here.

Make the decision, buy the tickets,
board the plane and sit and sleep
in a kind of nowhere, never-land,
a kind of slow ringing in the air.

At last through the tiny window
first the water, then the landing lights appear.

I hear the whine of turbines
in the air above this room.

I do not hear the echoes
or the chimes that always linger
in the lives of all those people
that plane was bringing here.

Trenchworks

I do not need my father
to tell me what to write.
He told me stories that were
almost true.
He talked events around
until the ordinary
became a diamond
and diamonds exploded into space
like galaxies of light.

I dredge poems from the dungeons
below the castle keep – are smeared
with filth and mud and darkness
from sewers that feed the leprous
and the rank.

He's given me his family
and his race.
I'll take his blarney –
I'll use it as a bait
to catch the unimagined,
universal, labyrinthine
trenchworks of collective dark,
the networked tunnels of all the Vietcong,
the plummeting caverns
where his and every mind
fall and intertwine.

Tightrope Walking

The blank page silent
like a chasm
and there is no net.

The blue Parker
your only wire
to safety
or into space.

Measure its weight
balanced on your fingers,
across the hollow
of your thumb.

Words flower
like geometry, inch onto wires
taut with print,
syllables like nerves.

Phrases cling to your flesh
toes and feet test each vowel,
consonants like vertigo,
the abyss between each line.

The poem explodes
as applause
rolling up,
open mouths, breathless faces

and your eyes transfixed
by that still point
in the void,

the nothing
you didn't know
you were even
aiming for.

Eden Yet

As always
the desk lamp with its green shade
and the bright globe reflect
the brown lacquer of the old desk
I've had since childhood
and is the naked core
of Eden yet.

But here the serpent,
blank and white as death,
coils flattened innocently
as every unread page
of a novel based on myth.

Coil on coil and sheet on sheet
insinuates the carnal metal
into the guileless hand
so knowledge of the pen
rewrites paradise like a god
who decorates the artless page
with cunning lines of verse.

At Berry Station

Step onto the platform,
there like the great arch at Luna Park,
the narrow, almost human face,
the blue and yellow nose,
wide, sloping eyes
of a diesel, looming down
onto the station but stopped, no, moving
not even at walking pace,
easing like a liner into its berth,
fireman leaning out concentrating
on the silver cylinder, exchange the staff
for the next section, stationmaster
standing waiting, the new staff
held out ready for the swap,
so slowly, slowly, like an earthquake
frozen into time…

It's done. He waves, turns
and walks away. The locomotives
throttling up, throbbing into power,
moving faster even as they get to me,
twin 90 class diesel electrics, linked
in multiple, six thousand horsepower
like the plates of the earth
pulsing into motion.

They pass like mountains
and the endless army of wagons
riding, rolling faster, longer,
thirty, forty, like an invasion,
like a herd of mammoths
filing through a valley,
the aftermath of monsters
sliding into the past.

The Moss Vale Train

Once you're away from the city
no more overhead, no gantries
or clutter, just the clean mainline,
double-tracked all the way south
to Melbourne. Your train's a cool
cocoon connected only to the rails,
the caterpillar that creaks around curves,

that twists on the gravel snakeway,
smooth with steel, bracketed by
the cold montage of signals, cuttings,
concrete sleepers.
The diesel grinds
growling into the grades, purrs
downhill as if relieved of strain,
as the Southern Highlands glide by.

Unattached to circuitry or suburb,
rolling like celluloid, the train
spools away and you're audience
to this high, hard, croded land,
the fences and farms of a landscape
like an old movie faded now
to yellow and the washed-out green
of wind-dried grass, of scrub and hills,
there beyond the camera's track.
Outside your window, old landscapes
like a film screening for you.

The City and the Stars

Beyond the window, the night.
Beyond the night the city
in panicles of light.

Beyond the city, a universe
of galaxies and stars, the black hole
of extinction, the stellar furnaces
of creation, heat and life –
electrons that dance a thin corolla
around the scrum of the nucleus
and the flicker of photons
fired from stars that plunge
to crescendos of nothing,
the vertigo of infinity
and the limits of the mind.

From the darkened cabin
of a jumbo, look down
through forty thousand feet
of brittle air,
the cities of the Persian Gulf,
orange flowers of light,
as if in bending down from space
you gently snap
the petals and hold them
in the palm of your hand.

Beyond the window is the night.
Beyond the night is the city.
Only the city. Only the night.

Disappointment

It didn't happen.
You hadn't seriously expected it
but hoped despite experience and sense
that it just might. Why not?
This time you could get lucky
but you told yourself you wouldn't
and you were right – no cause
for disappointment, yet to see
hope squashed lifeless
is a kind of loss – we live in hope
and when hope dies…

But really you've lost nothing, you're no worse off
though there's a sense of having missed
an improvement to a world
that'll have to battle on, mediocre as before.
Forget the great achievements
that didn't have to not occur –
the girls who never would say yes,
the prizes that went narrowly to someone else,
the jobs you almost got
except you were second on the list…

It's like a magic novel you haven't read –
the last copy gone minutes before you found the shelf,
the romance of a glittering life –
excitement, glamour and success,
crammed so full of grand events
that never almost happened
but in a brilliant dream of fiction
they dead-set did.

The Winds of August

Winter slides to spring.
The air thickens.
Warmth seeps into 6 a.m.
and the morning promises
vigour and renewal.

June and July struggled
through dismal into now,
a fetid tunnel
callous with graffiti,
ill health, discomfort, pain.
Mid-winter and the age of sixty.
Blood pressure's normal,
blood glucose and cholesterol
still far too high.

But now the winds of August
are breathing
something like passion
into the gathering season.
Confidence and energy build
towards the year's rebirth.

I walk with purpose
across Prince Alfred Park
towards the church tower
on the hill, where Cleveland
crosses Regent Street.
The traffic purrs
into the morning sun.

Morning's Symphony

It's not like a movie at all –
darkness and then the sudden
illumination of colours,
images, a story that more or less
makes sense. It's like an orchestra
tuning up – bits and pieces of sound,
the radio's on, later it's the TV
and the kettle. You've felt the shaking
of the bed and sense you wife's absence,
the awareness of lights on somewhere
in the house – bathroom, kitchen. But
your eyes aren't open and nothing's
making sense, until she says, 'It's
5.30' and puts the steaming tea
beside the bed.

       It's only then you feel
any of the elements coalesce
and the overture begins. The razor
glides through soap – splash your cheeks
and eyelids with cold, brisk water.
Make the bed, replace the furry toys
tumbled in their basket on the top.
(My god, two big jobs done and I'm
hardly up.) Get dressed – trousers, shirt,
sit on the bed for socks and shoes,
keys and change from the bedside table,
your wallet and pen taken from the desk,
grab your bag, load your lunch, then off.

Follow the score written for this
and every day and yet, what if,
this morning you just improvise –
not the normal trudge to the station
but this afternoon, dinner
and a movie straight from work. Take
the car and park halfway between
the theatre and a different station.

Its like a new, amazing song,
cool as the sea, a thin mist
feathers down the street you've got
entirely to yourself, trees and shrubs
in a melody of secrets
and the strange folk tunes of gardens.
Each parked car glistens in the coils
and webs of a moist, almost-night.
Each window's unique in the mystery –
dark panels to a stranger's life.
Down the wide hill's railway vista,
the breath and harmony of houses
on their second floors. The small,
end-stopped, corner hotel, crescendos
of stillness and the soft, clean notes
in early walking somewhere else.
A whole, new morning's symphony
in the world. Of you being there.

Headlines

Neanderthals still survive
in our minds, in dreams and shadows –
Bunyip, Yeti, Big Foot –
the not quite human ape,
we feared, despised and killed.

'Exterminate the brutes.'

Cannibals without speech,
without morality.
We study their bones.
They're here – race memories,
a nervousness about the past,
unease about the future.

And when the super-humans come?

When we flutter in the sideways radar
of their eyes, when
they handle our bones.

Electronic headlines flash:
THE LAST HUMAN IN CAPTIVITY DIES.

'An Ice Age hunter,
only half-evolved
towards intelligence; clever
but seldom wise.'

Pluto

In 2006 the International Astronomical Union downgraded the classification of Pluto from planet to dwarf planet. There could be over two hundred others in our solar system.

I am not alone here.
There are others – Vesta,
Haumea, Eris.
Soon there could be many others.
Sedra, Orcus, Quaoar
are also here waiting.
Some are larger than me,
most are not.

You've known I am here
only eighty years –
the ninth planet
but I am not
significant to you now.
Here in the Kuiper Belt
nothing is.
Your imagination shudders
into stillness here
and your knowledge dreams itself
to silence.

Charon is the queen
of the night,
my partner
in our binary system,
here in the void
where so many dwell
beyond Neptune
on the very edge of light.
Her mass is not
insignificant to mine.
We dance at arm's length.
We circle your sun
once every two and a half
centuries.

You have reassessed me.
I am not your planet anymore.
Like a rejected lover
I am now a dwarf
but still I am here.
I have always
been here.

You know so little of me.
I know nothing of you
nor care.

Angels Embracing

A painting by Nadine Sawyer

The embrace of angels
and the flight of birds –
rainbow colours, bodies curve
like butterflies, see
the lovers twisting down
weightless under wings, take
the female like a garland,
restraint and coyness
in her glance, she almost
kisses him, reaching up
he takes her like a prayer.

All is spirit,
delicacy and grace,
the blink of an eye,
wayward angels made of light,
ephemeral as the wind
but the carnality of birds,
breasts and buttocks
and the lost, determined
gaze of lovers swept
by stars and blood,
halfway between the apes
and angels we embrace
fragility and air, we
lust for heaven in their
legs and thighs and lips.

We hold the phoenix to our chests,
dance among the flames,
burn with skin and earth.
God is in our yearning
for the other,
for our bone and breath.

This Church

An upturned boat, its ribs and beams,
wooden polished arches and plates construct
the roof of this small church.

In stained glass the deepest blue of the sky
surrounds the Virgin and the child,
a voyage into life. At the altar

Christ crucified glows against
a rising sun, as if the stations of the cross,
build towards rebirth, a clear blue heaven,

as if the hollow of an empty church,
rows of empty pews, prefigures
all creation, the singularity,

a universe that erupts into dark matter,
energy's darker flow, gravity's ocean,
the mystery of the void. Our tiny rock

rotates forever around a lonely sun
in an outer spiral arm of a galaxy
whose voyage into the emptiness

we hardly feel across the swell
of time and space. This church, the upturned boat,
here on the ocean's edge of eternity.

The *Californian*

Ice creates mirages and mysteries.
No captain drives his ship
knowingly into ice so
the *Californian*, Leyland Line, bound
Liverpool to Boston, Stanley Lord,
her master, prudently stopped engines
for the night, somewhere south of the Grand Banks,
he'd blundered into the loose margins
of pack ice… 'Helm hard right,
engines full astern!' and spent the darkness
surrounded by an ice field,
that drifted miles further south
than anyone expected that season,
mid-April, 1912.

Twenty minutes to midnight, a large ship
its lights blazing as if Lady Luck
had laid bright fingers on her,
perhaps ten miles, perhaps south and east,
moving fast, driving hard towards New York
and to hell with whoever gets in her way.
Only one of *Californian*'s officers
thought he saw a liner – Lord imagined
a freighter, moving not so fast,
a ghost ship, whose shape and size and speed
was changed by the observer, as if
it wasn't really there at all.
Another ship, its port navigation light
blazing red in the distance, moving east?
What exactly was out there? How far? Where?

A radio message, *Californian* to *Titanic*:
'Three large icebergs just five miles north of you',
but no reply, later 'Shut up! Shut up!
you're jamming my signal. I'm busy.
I'm working Cape Race' – the new toy, radio
messages to friends, the great ship blasting out
across the night, more vital than the whine
of freighters paralysed in fear
of frozen water, 1912, the early days
of radio at sea, so eleven-thirty
and *Californian* closed down her radio,
her only operator went to bed –
on duty straight for fifteen hours,
and Lord, his ship now safe, also slept –
the usual command, 'Wake me if anything unusual occurs',
his masthead lights lit, his officers on watch,
steam in the boiler but otherwise the ship shut down,
drifting, sleeping among the ice,
going nowhere, no risk of collision.
Other ships also drifting, fear of growlers,
pack-ice, bergs, all safe in the night,
waiting for daylight to show lanes and pathways,
safe water between the teeth that open
rows of rivets, grind plates and inflict the wounds
that welcome in the sea, kill ships.
Californian was always safe from that.

Not so *Titanic*, her passengers and crew,
sunk at two-thirty, her forward plates
buckled by a berg, her new rivets sprung
and fifteen hundred people drowned.

Signals sent by morse to a strange ship
for one and a half hours, but the steamer
hurtled on, her lights growing dimmer,
as if listing as she turned away, perhaps
towards the horizon. 'Her lights looked queer',
Second Officer Stone, 'She looks very queer…
a big side out of the water…everything
was not right with her', but two o'clock,
assumed she'd stopped for the night, or turned south
away from the ice and left the area, gone.
Survivors claimed they saw a dark ship,
a few miles off, that didn't move
or help. Did they see *Californian*
so close against the cold, the North Atlantic
strange, unmoving, flattened by ice
that tricks the eyes that what appears so near
is miles away, the distant seems so close
and distance here is meaningless as stars,
or did they see *Mount Temple*, *Virginian*,
Saturnia, Birma, Samson or *Thistledhu*,
all drifting, all trapped as if the ice
had claimed them too.

At midnight, white rockets seen to the south,
rising no higher than the masthead lights
of a ship, but whose masthead, which ship?
What other dark ship seen from *Californian*,
her masts and spars like a skeleton in the night?
Behind her, below the horizon, six or eight rockets.
Titanic's flares rose high above her masts
and rigging but burst in a shower of coloured balls,
beautiful to see, terrifying from the sloping deck.
Lord remained in his cabin, his officers too scared
of his bad temper, reported nothing about the flares,
claimed he asked, half asleep, 'What is it?'
was satisfied all the flares were only white – sleep, cold,
confusion of colours, conventions, sleep…

Three-thirty, more flares but far to the south –
Carpathia racing up from the south-east,
her radio on all that night, listening helpless
as *Titanic* sank, help arriving hours too late,
but arriving. At last, two hours later,
Californian, her radio on duty now,
alert to danger, raising steam, picking
through the ice, moved west, then turned south to skirt
the western fringe of ice-field, surged to where
Titanic should have been and wasn't.
Frantic now, eyes strained for any sight
of survivors or boats or any life at all,
turned away north-east to meet *Carpathia*,
a voyage of three hours, twenty, thirty miles
through ice that could have sunk his ship.
Carpathia, distraught with all survivors,
steamed slowly away to New York, left Lord
to search, who found only scattered wreckage,
empty lifeboats on a flattened sea. Nothing else.

The enquiry and Lord was eviscerated –
he was close, six miles, could have rendered
assistance, could have come, ignored the flares,
ignored the radio, left them all to drown.
Lord maintained his position – twenty miles to the north,
his ship's top speed thirteen knots, hours away,
no captain orders top speed at night, no captain
risks the ice. He didn't even know she'd sunk
was even in distress – twenty miles
at thirteen knots – *Titanic*'s first flare
at midnight, sank at two-twenty, three hours
hard steaming or more. The enquiry
eviscerated Lord, who left the court
and his job, muttered to all who listened,
'At least I never drove my ship
at twenty knots, straight into an iceberg.'
A captain's first duty was and is
always the safety of his own ship.

Three quarters of a century later,
the wreck of *Titanic* found, thirteen miles
further south than she'd reported,
frantic among the panic and the chaos,
her officers forgot the Labrador Current
pushing south, mistook by their dead-reckoning
her latitude. *Californian* had stopped
thirty miles away, couldn't see *Titanic* –
well below the horizon, shouldn't even have seen
her flares, couldn't come in time anywhere
near her in clear water and there was no clear water.

No captain drives his ship
knowingly into ice. Ice creates fear,
mirages, mistakes, ruins lives,
kills ships.

Downstream

Our ferry's wake like moon shadow
tumbles away in silver, dances
in turmoil, chums and dazzles
in the rays of the yellow sun.
Symmetrical and parallel,
waves cascade towards each lush
and sliding bank, as if to mark,
with a wet commotion, our slow passage.
Behind, the river's glittered reach
narrows to an afternoon's confusion
of sun and land and indistinct.

Ahead, a spreading blue and grey,
the channel marked with beacons, green
and red, that opens up before us
a wider river – precise bays
and sweeping bends, the wind that hums
in from the sea, the great, grey bridge
delicate on its narrow piers,
a thin gate of concrete and flight. Beyond
the silent mangroves, a port of silos
and gantries, reduced and scattered
like untidy children's tiny toys.

Water

Always felt so comfortable near water,
in it or on it, sometimes even
below it. The surf, the tilt of a rock platform,
the ferry and the swell of the sea, the spray
under skysail or the thick vibration
of diesels through the hull, swimming laps.

A moon-child, at ease with the tides
of time and tears, sensual as the night,
sensitive as drifts in the warm Gulf Stream currents.
Born in Cancer, the cardinal of water signs
creates a refuge in serenity
where channels tidy the crust of the earth
I direct the flow quietly like a sluice.
If enraged, water overpowers the world
in flood-burst, surge and silt, wavecrest, berserk
as the sun, powerful as blood.

More carnal even than that, luxurious
the pleasure of amniotic fluid,
the warmth of being wrapped, more viscous
than the thin platitudes of air and wind,
more comforting than clothes, tighter than skin.
Water's like a blanket, erotic as a pulse,
a bloodstream flux, salt and smooth as the tide.
Return to the red womb, the ebb and neap
of nutrients, connection to all of that
great otherness, a floating universe
holds inviolate the clockwork heartbeat,
related galaxies of flesh and space.
Return to the womb, return to the sea.

Take a bath, relax inside another skin,
a body of water nourishes and clings.
Listen to your pulse, your own heart waves,
the thump of footsteps, windows bellow, doors
collapse, magnified in the tub's hydrology,
the scrape of chairs an earthquake's submarine
reverberation, seismic catastrophes
in an ocean trench and voices on the radio are
the vast songlines of humpbacked whales
and their creation myths, the birth of flow.

Dolphins were land animals that returned to the sea.
We're all nine-tenths water, anyway.

The Noise the Silence Makes

Listen to the noise
the silence makes:
a dog barking far away,
a bird chattering to itself,
the rumbling of the creek
as clouds clatter in from the west
and the rocks of the escarpment split,
the tableland sliding
down to the valley
that's V-shaped, as water
eats into the earth,
millimetre by millimetre,
century after century,
fluid and slow
the flow of the earth
towards the sea.

Rain and water,
water and rain.
Old silver gums
spread to the sky,
reaching into space
as below, the damp earth
fattens their roots
and the grass murmurs
in the sun.

A jet spools into flight,
spreads its wings over the bay
and out to sea,
a wide turn to starboard
to cross the coast
and pass to the north
as long thunder,
ten minutes out of Sydney
and climbing.

White trails of vapour
dissolving in the vacancy of air.
An hour to Melbourne,
the sky washed and blue
as pastel, tired,
nondescript like the morning
and superficial as silence.

Old Ships

1

How many were there? This a memory
hazed by a breeze, gusts chipping at wavelets,
lost in eddies, the flow of calendars
and diaries, thunderstorms and sunlight,
tides and pools, in minutes, months and years.

After school, wandered up through Figtree
into the bush, real bush then,
snakes and ticks, the tracks ill-defined
and overgrown, to Tarban Creek.
A group of us, how many? When?
The old ships anchored in rows,
strange, magnetic denizens of our
suburban, boyish world.
The beached carcasses of whales,
decayed mammoths, remnants from a war
I thought could never touch me then,
or ever, but realise now
it carved my life like fate.

2

From the tales my father told, battles
against the Japanese, air attacks,
laying mines in seaways far away,
in countries I'd never heard of then,
so fifty years later failed to comprehend
my friend's attraction to old films,
authentic yes, documentaries yes,
clichéd footage, stuff I'd grown up with
and didn't want to see again.
The kamikaze wheeling mast-high overhead,
machine-gunned by the frantic, twisting
gun crew, plummeting, burning,
a deadwood torch beside the ship,
an arm's length away, the pilot dead
for nothing,
or the crippled Grumman Wildcat
that smacks the crowded, wooden deck,
a US carrier, wheels collapsed, lurches,
careers among the rows of planes
and spinning sets them all aflame.
How old was the boy who died in that?

3

My parents married, dad not long released
from the air force that provided him
the cigarettes he'd die from sixty years later
and me, the post-war baby boom,
a free, university education
but then exactly the legal age to fight
the Vietcong, another right-wing waste
of lives, the direct result of World War Two.
Conservatives who ruled Australia
and its states, for twenty years
just loved a war to prove
how loyal they were to the USA, while
conscripted Australian boys of twenty
died for Uncle Sam in a country
they couldn't find on any map.
The idiots all said,
'We've got to fight them over there
or else we'll have to fight them here,'
as they rehashed the lessons learned
in a previous war, confusing both
China and Vietnam with newfound friends
the Japanese, all Asian, all the same
according to the knuckleheads in 1965.

4

The old ships, sea creatures like the old gods,
abandoned, derelict on a silent shore.
I knew nothing else of them
but somehow they were there,
like the carnage I knew had torn
the century in half just before my birth.
In adulthood I understood
the why and what they were –
old Bathurst class corvettes,
all purpose maids of naval work,
sweepers-up of mines, coastal escort ships,
Australian-built – *Benalla*, *Ararat*,
Gympie, *Bundaberg*, *Latrobe* or *Strahan*?
Which of the sixty had I seen?
I'll never know their names,
laid-up, left to rot in rows
before the final scrappers torch.
The Japs got most of them
commercially in the end.

A world war cast the darkest shadows
on my life. I've lived
for sixty years to pay
its subtle, terrible, extended price.

Journey to the Renal Ward

Like a hundred hospital orderlies
(is it training for the job?)
he talks incessantly of nothing much,
the weather, football, I don't know.
I'm sort of listening – my mouth
seems to make some kind of answer
but I'm alert to other things.

He hooks the drip machine behind the bed,
cages me here, releases the brakes, tugs me
out of Emergency and pushes
through the ward. I'm looking at the ceiling.
I turn to watch the walls slide by,
neutral creams and beige, colours of nothing.

We float in a labyrinth of corridors.
Wide, plastic doorways, sudden-angled turns,
the fluorescent atmosphere of midnight.
Rows of rooms and cubicles, flood-lit,
the nurses' stations, unmanned and abandoned.
Closed wards, stripped of life, empty now of pain,
the oppression of anxious desolation
in sharp focus, surreal and out of place
like the walls that cast no shadows, a painting
by Magritte, Chirico's great monoliths of stone,
sun-stark, ghost-lit, artificial middays
all solidly, forever, standing there.
They're waiting, wide acres of nowhere,
hallways of clear but not for me
and not tonight.

My orderly is talking of something.
I think I'm answering but I'm aware
of subterranean lakes, all swept with silence.
A lift leads to steel and glass, a stairwell,
black and looking out on blackness
and windows looking down on blackness.
Turn to a thin-lit refuge, sleeping ward
that seems our destination and our port.
My boatman guides me in, hooks me to another drip,
says goodbye, hands me over to the night-shift nurse.
End of a journey that's led me back in circles
to somewhere I know but have never known before,
via the halls of nowhere, the hauntings of the lost.

It was only later I remembered this:
I'd seen the tunnels and the underpass
to the fresh necropolis they've dug, beneath
our nightmares, down the inner suburbs of
every modern city and its midnight hells.

Respiratory Ward

Every breath's
liking heaving blocks
of concrete.

The long grind
against gravity
and ten per cent
lung capacity,
his mouth and muscles
strain to haul
enough to stay alive.

My father,
oxygen mask, the monitor
beside his bed –
fine filaments
of almost nothing,
staccato beats
link to a thin
rhythm of air
and everything there is.

The end of the ward,
his bed, his window-crossed
venetians.

Looking south
past plants and gardens,
clouds and space,
a world of trees
giddy with oxygen,
great, gathering crescendos
of breathless, pure,
priceless air.

Blood Test

Deep maroon, between brown
and purple, a Cabernet
heavy with blackcurrant
and tannin, viscous like jam.

When the syringe pierces
and taps the vein,
something flows like wine,
the dark pressure
of the heart,
the thin veneer of skin
and the chambers
of breathing.

It's a stain
disperses into air
like music sprayed
across the foyer
of an empty theatre,
wasted in the glass.

Kidney Stone

Geography narrows
to the hospital bed.
The metal narrows
to flintstone shards
knifed in your side,
slow and rhythmic
grinding.

The mind narrows
to a minute scale.
Intricate, precise
contour maps
of blood and flesh
calculate
the topography of pain.

Tectonic plates,
continents of bone
drag your nerves
and ridges grate
inside your veins.

A nurse wraps
plastic around your arm,
blood pressure, pulse,
and slips the metal
under your tongue.

Calderas cough
in the morphine valleys
of the night.

This is not
the age of iron,
this new stone age,
shards and grit.

The world narrows
to flint.

A. Cooke

30.12.22, a police mugshot

Alice Adeline Cooke, were you twenty then?
Why were you arrested – what crime
near the end of that forgotten year, a city
we'd hardly recognise or understand.
What did they charge you with? Theft?
Prostitution? No – your shirt's too workaday for that.
Murder? You look too calm, too normal
but if murder, who did you kill? And why?

You don't look hardened but I could be wrong.
An ordinary face I've often seen on trains
or in the street, not beautiful but there's no sign
of evil, no deformity or ugliness.

Your glance is frank, direct towards the camera,
forthright, curious though vaguely masculine.
Untidy hair tied back in a messy kind of part.
A firm-set mouth, serious determined jaw.
You're facing prison. How long did they lock you away?

It's a face unmarked, unlined except the eyes –
large, unblinking, though one seems slightly wider
than the other, as if something's not quite right,
but then you'd hardly notice that
in the concentrated blaze of stare,
as if there's some overwhelming question
you were asked then, that must be answered now.

Autumn and Darkness

And autumn moves with heavier clothes.
The sleeves of your winter jacket
cover scars on your upper arms,
the tattoo behind your shoulder
and the deeper curve of your breast.

The burning flesh of summer
smothered you down to the bone
and the overcoats of winter
warm the blood but leave you after
naked and alone.

April starts with a day of fools
and ends with the gathering dark.
You've scoured your flesh with the razor again.
The longer sleeves of your jacket punish
your bandaged lower arms.

Autumn and darkness, skin and bone,
the shock of the sharper season,
the warmth of blood beneath the blade.
Your clothes are dressings that daily bind
the wounds of your jagged mind.

The Tango Dancers

A photograph by Sharrukina Malek

There's a blurring of the real –
apartment blocks and towers
tilt to them.
The tango dancers oblivious,
breathe for each other,
move only for the other.

Eyes glower into hers,
black hair salt and peppered
with the formality
of cruel, the elegance
of contempt,
his snarl of lips,
profiles of hate – her body's
ritual and will.

She smiles,
a vertigo of submission,
the fetters of trust –
naked muscles in her back
and arms that cling
like spasms.
The sensuality of pride,
the passion of power.

Oblivious the lacerations
of their love,
he frowns her into beauty
and dances her to grace.

The unreal city's
glass and steel
bend to their fantasy
like willows.

Two Young Soldiers

For John Joseph Egan and Fredrick Raggatt

Sepia portraits of two young soldiers
in different uniforms from World War One.
The older in a tailored jacket, his gloves rest
on a cane, officer of the British Army.

Handsome, confident, a self-conscious almost-smile.
The younger stands in boots, hands behind his back,
a shapeless tunic, his face blank, a boy
with eyes lowered, anxious, vulnerable and lost.

1916 and Fred is twenty-two,
Jack barely in his middle teens. Impossible
to read their fates from faces, stance or uniforms?
Different armies. Different lives.

Jack, working class, Australian, died of mustard gas
and heavy labour, early thirties, while Fred,
I remember well, who gently passed away
at eighty-four – my other father, Pop.

Two young men whose very different lives
the Great War ripped apart – my grandfathers,
though Jack lived for me only in my father's memory.
Both served in France though never met and later

lived in Sydney suburbs – Auburn, Carlton.
Impossible to read their fates from photographs?
I'm not so sure of that. I'm told
that of the two, I more resemble Jack.

Snake Lady

You're fascinated by snakes, once had
a diamond python as a pet.
You wear your snakes of gold in rings
around your fingers. I admire them,

stroke them, as I admire real snakes,
their sheer horizontality,
their loops and flow, their tongues flicking,
their reptile eyes searching

but always my black revulsion at
something beautiful that can kill.
I've never touched a snake.
The ring you gave me and I wear

is weighty, masculine and gold,
has a coiled snake in one corner.
I love it as I love you.
I stroke it as I think of you.

Once, planting a shrub under an old tree,
underground a cable, solid as my arm.
I threw back the soil in horror –
a red-bellied black, hibernating but deadly.

Your ring is a snake around my finger,
symbol of healing, symbol of death, the earth.
You are curled around my heart. I love
your rings, the blackness of your hair.

For Panadda

You're elegant and delicate and sweet.
I fear for you, exotic and too gentle
for routine roughness in the world's rough trade,
our brash and everyday brutality.
I've loved your sharp, ironic tease, your sense
of fun, near collapse with childlike laughter
and profuse regrets, should playful barbs
inflict a wound. You're sorry far too much.

I've taught the English words, phrases you find
so funny to practise, that let you sound
dangerous and tough. I hope you'll spit them
catlike if you need to fight, you're actress
enough, my teaching's good enough to see
my 'deer' out-stare hyena packs, and laugh.

Gin and Tonic

A tinkle of diamond ice
knocking and nicking
the bottom, crashing together,
locked tumbling in the lens
of a long, cool glass.

Two spits of gin – be generous
and spurt from the shaker.
Thicker, clearer than water,
the tang of juniper and barley,
astringent to the tongue,
the tingle of the scent
in tangled worlds of dry
and sweet, spices, harems,
the exotic, far-off east.

Then the tonic – springs
of sharp, wells of cool
and the quench of quinine.
A naughty fizz
displays her sexy lemon-rind.
She winks an eye, pouts
pole dancing on a straw
and purrs, 'Taste me, sip me.
Oh, drink me now.'

Who Did You Say?

I never feel more alive
than when I hear
Leonard Cohen sing
'Who by Fire?'

The depths of baritone
and the thrill of guitar
plucked across my nerves –
the exotic, the haunted,
the strange.

And the song.
This yearning
in syllables
of wordbeat and time,
the creation and the quickening.

It's a song about death
and the myriad ways
to die.

'And who did you say
was calling?'
And who is it
who's dying?

All of us, of course,
but first the notes seduce the ear,
synapses lulled
and the heartbeat quickened.

The whimsy of the hood
and the scythe
among the dancers
and the dance.

Floating

Floating out of sleep
when sleep's creeping away,
where there are pools
of blue wakefulness
still swamped in sleep's wash
and undertow
your mind's also drifting
into a world

not exactly
like the life you lead,
more like strings
intersecting into somewhere else
whose logic develops
with slight complications,
then just peters out
to nothing, as if,
'keep it simple stupid'

applies to dreams
that also cannot tolerate
too much reality
even when you're floating
into another world
that's partly your own.

Time

It's four in the morning.
Unable to sleep, I sit
in the sheltering darkness of my room,
gaze out to where the summer leaves
of the great tree are sheets of blackness
between me and the faint streetlights beyond.

In a splutter of wings, a sudden currawong
solidifies on a branch and sits
savouring the darkness too, just feet
from my open window. I could reach out
and touch it, stroke the blackness of its night.

Then it's gone, enveloped by something
I cannot see but I know is there.
Not a sound, no cars pass, hours before dawn
and the new hum of human urgency.
I am at one with myself and the night.

There is time to be a rock.
There is time to be a deep, dark pool
and there is time to be the wind.
It's four in the morning, unable to sleep.
This is time just to be.

The Song

Your grown-up children both
think you're a staid old thing.
You don't drink, don't eat meat,
don't sing.

You look severe, learned, determined,
you're always at work or reading.
That's what they think.

But I've seen you dance wildly
like a twelve-year-old,
joke and giggle, pleased or excited.
You hurl away inhibitions,
whirl into life like a carnival,
relishing the pleasure.

Yes, I love your darkness, your mystery,
but more, I love the little girl
who's playing hide and seek
with me, behind your smile.

And when you laugh
with helpless glee,
in a torrent of mirth and banter
I'm brave and young and strong.
That's what you do for me.

Behind the serious woman,
the child,
behind the child,
the song.

Joe Lynch   1927

'…and this one life
Of Joe, long dead, who lived between five bells'
                              Kenneth Slessor, 'Five Bells'

Away from the lights of the Quay, the ferry
skirts the brick tram shed, dark as a castle,
Bennelong Point, and pushes the evening
into vast rips of darkness as the harbour,
almost black, shudders in the wakes of work boats
and pleasure. Water and wind smack against the hull,
the hiss of steam pumping into pistons,
the thump and thud of cylinders, bells
vibrate in the harbour, the wind, the night.

The ferry's crowded with laughter and expectation.
It's Saturday and every seat's taken,
pressed shoulder to shoulder, hip to hip.
There's the chirping of girls and the deeper
certainties of men, dressed for parties
and warmth in overcoats and white scarfs
over their formal suits and coral bright,
the evening gowns of ladies, shoulders wrapped
in furs, their tight hands elegant in gloves.

'Deep and dissolving verticals of light…'
The long, dark finger of Cremorne Point.
A few flickers, the wharf, the distant flares
of houselights and sparks from trams. Light beckons
across the night and Joe Lynch, dark in dark,
dressed as an artist should, bohemian and odd,
a black and white cartoonist, his shrewd
and witty nips against the middle class
and loud pretensions of the insincere,
is wrapped in an old raincoat against the cold,
greasy, unwashed, buttons off, the bulge of pockets
and beer bottles pushed deep in every one.
The party in Mosman, the music, laughter, girls.

Joe's tall and thin, he of the 'gaunt chin'
and the 'pricked eye', raging against
…well, everything, red hair standing up, grinning
his pure, wide Irish smile.
Mischievous, proud,
he's perched on the railing, the lower deck,
feet not touching anything and his coat
billowed by the wind but weighted hard
to his body, slender with beer bottles,
his hands loose and free, riding the harbour
and the conversation. Joe's laughter
stirs their laughter like a song.

                    Then it doesn't
...a slight lurch, the wash of a passing ferry.
'Waves with diamond quills and combs of light
that arched their mackerel-backs'...then nothing.

The long ache of absence, 'the eyeball press'
of water, 'the thumbnail push', 'the eardrum crack'
and Joe lost in 'the pygmy strait', a few
feet of water, enough to split the living
and wash away the dead...your body, Joe
was never found.

Slessor's elegy for Joe, was twelve years later,
his bones 'long shoved away and sucked away
in mud' and still the distant bells
for the most recent dead, bells that mark
the passing of the minutes into hours,
'the flood that does not flow', but moves
the living ever closer to the dead.

All quotations from, and references to, 'Five Bells' by Kenneth Slessor

Walking to Redfern

Regent Street dog-legs over Cleveland,
three directions down, traffic,
Don't Walk signs but somehow here
there's soul. Old terraces in rows
lean sideways down a falling road.
Assured and horizontal, drumbeat
footsteps push you up the hill.

Heartbeats link themselves
to earth – shoes that grip and cling.
Here's a rhythm sacrificed
finality to future and a place.
Your mind reacts to landscapes here,
your spirit's floating, explores the park,
commits a trespass into buildings and their yards,
sings within the trees. Let your breathing
count the seconds, pump the hours away.
A candle in the dark, the standing stones
that glower from the summit of a hill.

Walk within the yellow wood
where paths divide and circle back
to someone's vision of the future,
the subtlety of there.
The city falls behind. Move downhill,
the place that's here, the place you're going to,
the everlasting ebb, the new coordinates
of time. My body's walking here,
my spirit floats the lower streets of there.
I walk on through, merge myself in time.

www.ingramcontent.com/pod-product-compliance
Lightning Source LLC
Chambersburg PA
CBHW070924080526
44589CB00013B/1418